Failure is Success

By Michael Kedman

Contents:

Working towards success is one of the most challenging commitments a human can face, proven to have a grave impact on someone's physical and mental health. A never-ending test because of the amount of failure that is likely to occur. Once the dream, vision or goal has been achieved, there is almost a feeling of instant relief as supposed to a celebration. When desires to achieve visions are ocean deep, they can haunt an individual daily. The heavy fear of failure causing distress, insomnia and most of the enjoyment drained, purely because of the suffers along the journey.

However, thankfully there is hope!

Throughout this read, I'll aim to give the key components needed to make your journey of success more enjoyable, with the simple aim of establishing the healthiest mindset to have behind the ambitions of succeeding. Steering our minds to an area of clarity whilst finding specific principles that are common among the 'successful'.

Blueprinting a simple guide put together to give this bumpy ride of success the best chance of being an amazing trip.

Failure

An act or instance of failing or proving unsuccessful; lack of success.

If the definition of failure reads a 'lack of success' and success is the accomplishment or aim of a purpose. Then failure is never permanent and can only ever seen as temporary.

The perspective of failure is subjective and therefore aspects that can be seen as negative can also be seen as positive. What we have to understand is that this is a huge part of the journey, allowing us to alter, adapt and build from our last experience.

Without failure, we cannot learn, and when we fail the experience is now an important step towards gaining wisdom.

Every field takes time to master, and in that time failure is a key component to develop and grow. Whilst growing, fresh challenges present themselves and having the courage to face them knowing there is a possibility of failure is success within itself. Yes, that failure might be a step backwards in accomplishment however it is a step forward in preparation like an arrow being pulled backwards for a launch that is even further into our visions.

"*Success involves going from failure to failure without a loss of enthusiasm.*"
Winston Churchill

Here is a noble example
Considered being one of, if not the greatest basketball player of all time, a young Michael Jordan was devastated when he was cut from his high school varsity basketball team in his sophomore year. Thankfully, he didn't give in to this 'failure'

and it only inspired him to put in more work towards improving his all-round game. This work ethic and perseverance lead him to win 6 NBA championships along with 6 NBA Finals MVP (most valuable player) awards and many other achievements.

"I have missed more than 9,000 shots in my career. I have lost almost 300 games. On 26 occasions I have been entrusted to take the game-winning shot, and I missed. I have failed over and over and over again in my life. And that is why I succeed"

Michael Jordan

Failure is a perspective, extracting lessons from failure is where we find our success. It's difficult to see the full picture when we are in the frame. Meaning from the inside looking out, it may be difficult to see the small progress, especially when we focus on the failures.

Having the desire to perform at the best of our abilities is a success itself, but it can become the pressure that can make us overly critical of ourselves. It's important we understand that this is all part of the process of development and try not to take any lack of progress personally.

As soon as negative thoughts enter our mind, we must see them as a test, with the belief that we can now use these negative thoughts positively by accepting that they are a natural part of the success process. When we use these thoughts as ammunition to face the next opportunity, we can enter it with the wisdom we have now gained, along with the energy that can prepare us for the next phase of our journey. Also, this time it will be different because we now have more experience.

For example, as a 100m sprinter at an international level, your job train and prepare for a race that will last under 11 seconds and finish the race as fast as you can. The smallest margins are a fine line between winning and losing. For instance, In the Beijing Olympics Usain Bolt broke the

100m record with a time of 9.69secs. The last-placed sprinter was Darvin Patton with a time of 10.03 seconds.

That can be the small margin between 1st and 8th place as a sprinter.

The first factor you face when sprinting is the start, leaving the blocks too early is a false start and in some races chances are as minimal as one false start and you're out of the race. The sport's governing body, the IAAF, has a rule that if the athlete moves within 0.1 seconds after the gun has fired, the athlete has false-started. They base this figure on tests that show the human brain cannot hear and process the information from the start sound in under 0.10 seconds.

meaning you can train for months or even years for a race, and it can all end in a split second because of a false start.

At that moment of being disqualified because of a false start, the negative emotions flood a sprinters mind.

With negative thoughts such as :

I've let everybody down

I've let myself down

The next race is far away

Here is a passage we can use as a reminder to ourselves after these thoughts emerge in a moment of 'failure' -

*This is my goal and I will do whatever it
takes to Achieve It
This was a lesson
I will learn from this failure and every
other failure coming my way
I will work smarter
I will adapt faster
I will work harder
and I will not quit until my dream is a
reality*

"I trained 4 years to run only 9 seconds. There are people who do not see results in 2 months, give up and leave. Sometimes failure is sought by oneself." Usain Bolt.

"You have to get comfortable with failure. You have to actually SEEK failure. failure is where all of the lessons are." - Will Smith

"Failure is a great teacher and, if you are open to it, every mistake has a lesson to offer." Oprah Winfrey

"Failure is an option here. If things are not failing you are not innovating." Elon Musk

Passion

It has several definitions, but the definition that aligns with success reads :

an intense desire or enthusiasm for something.

What is my passion?
A question we should ask ourselves throughout the years of working towards our goals. Writing it down and putting it somewhere visible to remind us daily. The primary passion is significant, however, the minor detailed passions within the primary passion are reminders of why you do what you do. Finding this deeper ignited fire from within helps drive the extra motivation we

*need during times of hardship. When we
think of what we want to achieve in our
vision and the impact it will have on our
family, friends and ourselves. We should
also question: Is this dream or goal large
enough to impact the world?. Is the journey
of success we are embodying a genuine
passion of ours?*

**Develop a passion for learning. If you do,
you will never cease to grow."
-Anthony J. D'Angelo**

*When passion is felt there is a strong
emotion and intense enthusiasm combined
giving us fuel. This fuel is the foundation of
our journey towards our visions. Finding*

our passion is identifying how a field makes us feel. The easiest way to find passion is by aligning our dream with something we love doing or finding our love within a field we are already talented in. Passion is something you can't fake, it's the energy that is found deep inside us, providing the will power to sacrifice with ease. Along your journey, you want your passion for your work to be recognised because that energy can be contagious and help open doors purely from the belief in you.

"People buy into the leader before they buy into the vision." John C. Maxwell

Passion is within the obsessive love for our craft once we have it, we must hold on to it and embrace it as it is the key to the strength needed along the tough times ahead. It should be the basis of why our work ethic towards what we want to achieve is endless.

"Passion is energy. Feel the power that comes from focusing on what excites you."-Oprah Winfrey

Resilience

The capacity to recover quickly from difficulties; toughness.

Throughout life, our psychological resilience is tested. We develop the ability to mentally or emotionally cope with a crisis at the earliest of ages, for instance, picture an infant falling whilst learning to walk for the first time. Their reaction to their first fall being a painful cry and they might feel the fear of falling again, discouraging them from having the next attempt however with the help of their parents eventually with time they can overcome this fear and build up the courage to walk with a newfound resilience.

Developing behavioural capabilities that allow us to stay calm in any crisis is a healthful practice that is always worth putting time into. We all have good and bad days whilst going through our share of crises. Our initial reaction shouldn't be our focus, the aim is to bring that energy down with an aim to choose to respond by remaining calm and rational because it is a healthier way to finding a solution because responding with anger, fear or any other negative emotion has a high chance of having a negative outcome for the main reason of not operating from a stressful state. Adopting full control of our reactions and actions is a skill within itself.

One way to practice is by using the three R's method by reflecting, resetting, and refocusing.

Reflection brings clarity when understanding ourselves. Once we understand our current selves thoroughly from our reactions to how and why we felt a certain way, then we can move on and work towards how we can improve. This is where we can start resetting, with more knowledge, and begin the process of starting again fresh. An exciting opportunity to apply what we have learned in the last stage of refocusing and then preparing for what is next.

The three R's is a healthy method for when things don't go as expected. A method that improves our ability to adapt and bounce back from a failure or even maintain after a successful experience.

We find an outstanding example of resilience within the story of Thomas Edison in his invention of the light bulb. According to the legendary inventory, he made thousands of versions of the incandescent light bulb before he got it right And since the prolific inventor was granted more than 1,000 patents, it's easy to picture him indirectly testing his resilience daily in his lab through his attempts to improve lives for us all with his astounding inventions and the amount of resilience he had built to fight off the negative discouragement of trying again after so many failures is incredible and in his invention of the light bulb proves the value of developing our resilience is a key factor in the journey of success.

'Fall seven times, stand up eight,' - Japanese proverb

<u>Sacrifice</u>

"There is no progress or accomplishment without sacrifice." Idowu Koyenikan.

During a time where we are surrounded by new distractions daily from social media, social pressures, Television and the list goes on. The value of sacrificing for the greater *reward has risen, and it's become more difficult than ever before. There are many ways to divert our attention away from our targets, and this can be the fine line in determining if we can attain our visions. This can make or break. Sometimes, it might only hinder the levels of success we can reach however in most cases it's as severe as not achieving success completely. Sacrifice is the fee we have to pay for success. Becoming comfortable feeling uncomfortable for however long it takes in a leap of faith to achieve this vision we desire most.*

"Let us sacrifice our today so that our children can have a better tomorrow.". - A. P. J. Abdul Kalam

The first steps to preventing this from happening are identifying what to sacrifice. Below is a list put together of common sacrifices among some great success stories that can make a vast difference in increasing our chances of seeing results along our journey of success.

Time –
One of the most important sacrifices. In "Outliers," in 2008 Malcolm Gladwell wrote that "ten thousand hours is the magic number of greatness."
The core meaning behind this, in theory, is clear to be considered elite and truly

experienced within a certain craft. You must practice it for ten thousand hours.

Ask yourself:
How am I spending my time?
Have I prioritised enough time for my targets today?
What is my daily routine?

Leisure - even when we love what we are doing, sometimes we may need a break. Hanging out with friends, taking part in a hobby or doing something outside of 'work' and taking some time to focus on enjoyable leisure activities can give a person's mind a rest from daily stress, which is important for mental and physical balance.

This is great for when it's time to refocus because our minds will operate from a restful state.

The key pillar is having balance and doing what works for you. Being truly honest with yourself because in the end, if you are not putting in the work, you are only cheating yourself.

With that being said everyone is different, we are all unique. What may work for one person might not work for someone else.

Being truly honest with yourself when asking these questions :

Have I done enough today towards working on my goals?

Is my work/play ratio where I want it to be?

Location - Sometimes sacrifice might be with stopping a habit or avoiding the wrong crowds, sometimes it might be as simple as relocating to a place with more opportunities to support your visions. This has worked for many successful people from actors, comedians moving to Hollywood to entrepreneurs, athletes, scholars moving away for a finer education. Wherever there might be more opportunities in their fields. This is a very common sacrifice and a decision that can affect someone's life for better or worse, however, something you can never know until it has been experienced. It takes courage and faith in your abilities to trust that being away from your support systems, surroundings, and family/friends is worth your desirable dreams.

The greatest lessons are opening your mind to whole new experiences.

Family & Friends

A sacrifice that has proven to be important can relay back to the saying 'Show me your friends and I'll tell you who you are' by Vladimir Lenin

Mindsets can be contagious, who we spend our time with daily can shape the mindset that we have therefore a direct effect on who we become. There are so many negatives and positives with friends and family, gauge whether someone is taking you away from the mindset you need to be in, then it is wise to keep your distance or completely cut them off. The most difficult thing is identifying this.

Having a healthy friendship group around you can be a catalyst for your successes, or at least for fun on the journey of your trip of success.

No road is long with good company.

-Turkish proverb

Here are some questions to ask yourself -
Does this friend uplift me and support my
visions?

How do I feel around this friend?

With a friend like this, can I see myself
reaching the heights of my potential?

When you've asked yourself these questions,
decisions have to be made at some point,
because avoiding certain friends or even
family members can be the slight difference
needed to put you right on the path of
attaining your dreams of becoming
successful.

Persistence & Perseverance

Persistence - the continued or prolonged existence of something
Perseverance -
persistence in doing something despite difficulty or delay in achieving success

When discussing Perseverance, I want to bring light to a story treasured across the word. The story of the Chinese Bamboo Tree This tree has a seed that is so solid that when planted, it will do nothing for around five years. Almost Nothing happens in the first four years. However, watering and caring for that seed throughout the four years is essential. That is all until the fifth year.

After five years of constantly caring to this seed and then 'Boom' the seed breaks through the soil and grows into a beautiful tree with a rate of growth recorded upwards of 3 feet a day, which is around 90 feet a month. You can stand there and watch it shoot up! (It has been timed at approximately one inch of growth every 40 minutes.)

This story of the Chinese bamboo tree aligns with persistence once said, if the person who planted the seed stopped watering and caring for that seed at any point, then that tree could not flourish with tremendous growth after that fifth year.

This can be a great analogy regarding perseverance, and this is the mindset needed whilst climbing the mountain of our success visions.

During that time, the perseverance used by the planter of the seed helped the tree reach its full potential, and this is an example of a way of thinking during this journey. On the days when things are difficult and circumstances may affect our motivation it's important, we understand that every moment of care and nurture is vital and has a direct effect on our growth. Take that energy we are putting into focusing on the negatives and using it as motivation to apply more work ethic.

Persistence aligns with perseverance, and when talking about Persistence, it's important to mention attitude.

Attitude is essential in so many ways. Here are three types of attitudes -

Positive, Negative, and Neutral

Positive attitude - being optimistic about situations, interactions, and yourself. People with positive attitudes can remain hopeful, seeing the best probable outcome even in difficult situations.

Negative attitude - Usually a pessimistic outlook on things, ignoring the good and focusing your attention on the bad in people, situations, events, etc.

Neutral attitude -
Meaning there is minimal doubt, neither is there any kind of hope. Tending to ignore the

problems in life. It is as if they don't think about anything that much and doesn't care for the same as well. They rarely feel the need to change themselves.

Attitude is a general way of understanding the personality of a person. Sometimes having the appropriate attitude doesn't always decide success, however, some patterns suggest having a positive mindset can be the best way to give someone an enjoyable, successful journey. The recipe for a positive attitude lies within gratitude. When you are grateful and appreciate the small things you have such as food, shelter and water. It's a reminder that there are things to be positive even in the times that seem the darkest.

Being able to identify with what mindset you are currently in is an important step in becoming self-aware, and self-awareness is a key component when striving to be persistent. Why do I want to achieve these goals?

What is my biggest motivation?

What are the repercussions of not achieving these goals?

Persistence is one of the most difficult things to maintain when we are trying to achieve anything in life.
Failure can be the 'kryptonite' of persistence. Meaning the more we fail, the more difficult it is to be persistent.

It takes a mentally strong individual to stay persistent through failure and that strength is in all of us because daily we wake up and face life itself.

The thought process behind failure for many might be in stages

for example

you've had an experience, and the outcome has not turned out as expected (stage 1), then you over analyse the situation with a pessimistic outlook

(stage 2) which can lead to negative predictions usually (stage 3)

Followed by excuses and a hefty amount of doubt. (stage 4)

Understanding that failure is a part of success is the key. Each time you fail, it gives you a new opportunity to learn from. Trial and error is a pivotal part of the process, and it's important to use the experience that you've gained through this failure to move forward and aim to avoid the same mistakes twice.

By tracking progress with an aim to making what you've practised, permanent. We are what we consistently do and consistency aligns with persistence. A very effective pair when combined.

Failing doesn't mean that I am worthless,
It doesn't mean I'll never achieve the things
I've set out to achieve

It's an opportunity to reflect and use as preparation what is next to come.

The man who says he can and the one who says he can't are both right Confucius (Chinese philosopher)

Self-Discipline -
when one uses reason to determine the best course of action regardless of one's desires

"A disciplined mind leads to happiness, and an undisciplined mind leads to suffering"– Dalai Lama

The rollercoaster of life is unpredictable things can take a turn for the worse at any point in time of the journey and vice versa. However, with self-discipline the mind can be at ease, being the foundation of a successful, happy life. We have the free will to have control over ourselves however we do not have control over others. Understanding that you can only have full control over your actions and choices, is a good way of recognising the importance of giving 100% in everything you do. Discipline helps provide rules to live your life efficiently and having discipline in your life can lead to the sacrifices you've made in the present to benefit you in your future. One way to add discipline is to create habits that turn into routines. This structures your time and can lead to the consistency to master your craft, and with time this can prepare you for an opportunity.

"You have power over your mind, not outside events. Realise this, and you will find strength."–Marcus Aurelius.

Minor principles/life choices we face daily can be the start, for example, when our morning alarm signals, waking up and getting out of bed is a difficult discipline. Daily it can trigger the mindset of a minor achievement that can then set the tone for other daily activities, giving us that boost in our step to desire accomplishing more. Enjoying the challenge of winning the minor battles of discipline put you in a position to be able to achieve anything you put your mind to.

"Without self-discipline, success is impossible, period."–Lou Holtz.

Self-discipline can be the foundations of a mindset that allow you to make fewer mistakes, bring more simplicity to your journey, and most importantly make it clear of the direction we aim to head in life. Every time there is a bump in the road of success, reverting to the amount of discipline along with habits and sacrifices made can be used as the anchors for the optimism and hope needed to continue with a prolonged sense of defeat. The mindset of it's not my time now as supposed to it will never be my time.

"Discipline is the bridge between goals and accomplishment."–Jim Rohn

Removing Doubt

Doubt - To be uncertain about (something): to believe that (something) may not be true or is unlikely.: to have no confidence in (someone or something)

Fear - the anticipation of the possibility that something unpleasant will occur:
For eg having grown up during the Great Depression, he had a constant fear of running out of money.

Feelings of self-doubt are a natural battle we are all likely to face on our journey towards our goals. Having true faith that 'whatever the mind can conceive and believe the mind can achieve' is a powerful mindset that can help clear our minds of this self-doubt and have while striving for success. It's difficult however if what we wanted to attain was easy then it wouldn't be as valuable.

The negative emotions that occur along the journey of success have a strong attachment to doubt. Some people use doubt to their advantage, and that fear of failure helps drives their work ethic. However, operating from this mindset is the easiest way to live a life without peace, plenty of added pressure and stress. True happiness can be found within having peace of mind. Also, the consistency of this mindset is a beautiful obstacle to achieve.

Becoming the master of their mind is a common goal among many of the successful. Neglecting the mental side of your development can have damaging effects in the long and short term. One way we can start working on or mindset (mental goals) is to write our thoughts down by brainstorming or bullet pointing. Providing a simple way of giving ourselves clarity and picking up on exactly where we are from a mental standpoint. Learning to only have 'winning' in our minds and never focusing on losing is a way to shift our minds to a place where doubt can be removed. This isn't a simple task however small habits and steps imprinted in your daily routine can help to be the catalyst of someone adopting this mindset.

Earlier, when touching on sacrifice, one of the common sacrifices is 'family and friends' and they can have a huge effect when aiming to remove doubt, this is a common issue faced by the journeymen/women of success. Our inner voice can be a guide to every action. We can control our thoughts, however, having the ability to control how we take in the opinions of others is a task within *itself. You may believe in something, and if anyone around you doesn't support that vision completely, it's important to distance yourself from them as a sacrifice for your vision. Doubt isn't only from within it is also a projection from external sources. Yes, we can use this as motivation however when it is coming from our sources of validation then it has undoubted effects. Time proves it wise to prevent these situations when they are discovered, rather than aiming to cure the situation when it might be too late. Yes, it can be seen as ruthless however these are the fine margins the successful will take.*

Here's a story paraphrased by George Couros

Two young boys were skating on ice when suddenly, one of them fell through and got trapped under. His friend started to punch the ice, hoping to break it, but could not get through. In desperation, the friend climbed a tree and broke off a huge branch, came back down the tree and started smashing the ice, eventually breaking it and miraculously saving his friend.

As emergency services came after the boy was safe, they sat in amazement and wondered how the little boy was able to break off the branch, smash the ice and save his friend. As they were sharing their amazement, an old man walked up and said, "the boy could do it because there was no one here that told him he couldn't"

This is a glorious reminder that as children our minds are capable of imagining the unimaginable, believing we can achieve anything we put our minds to.
As we age typically, the more our childhood dreams or beliefs are placed into question and this can be a result of the external doubt we are confronted with daily. Sometimes others project their fears onto us, they believe they can't achieve something and place that same doubt on those around them. No one should have the power of telling us what we are capable of because learning daily about ourselves and how is it possible

for someone else to know our full capabilities when they are forever developing throughout our life.

Having complete trust in our capabilities can be demanding. It's something that can be easily said, but not easily done.

Our confidence is tested constantly and not the confidence we show others but the inner confidence we have in our minds, ideally the way we view ourselves. Many failures are due to a lack of belief we have in ourselves, and sometimes this can even stop us from trying. As mentioned before having the courage to attempt anything whilst understanding there is a chance we may fail, is a genuine success itself.

Failing when we're fully focused, constantly pushing our limits and giving everything we can, combined with the full belief that it's only a matter of time until we succeed, is healthy in so many ways, especially because it helps us enjoy the process. We must have faith because faith allows us to fly with wounded wings. The energy behind the belief is powerful when backed by actions. We must find the belief deep in our hearts, removing doubt and any comparisons with others. Whether it's through religion, external motivations such as a mentor, or from within by just wanting better for ourselves. Resulting in changing our entire perception and outcome of our journeys.

"Faith gives you inner strength and a sense of balance and perspective in life."
Gregory Peck

Timing & Patience

For an event to happen in a specific way, numerous occasions need to occur prior. Many opportunities present themselves when least expected and trusting in the process while preparing is a key component of success and another way of saying 'Never give up'. When questioning why many successful people have attained the levels of success It's easy to bring 'luck' into the conversation.

What is luck?

Defined as the force that causes things, especially good things, to happen to you by chance and not as a result of your efforts or abilities.

With years of studying, training, researching or any other form of spending time working on a craft. Solely 'luck' cannot be used as the reason for why someone is successful, even a lottery winner had to put forth a ticket.

Nonetheless, 'Luck' can be seen as part of success. The timing of opportunities can sometimes be unpredictable however if you are preparing for an opportunity and it arrives. You've still had faith and put yourself in a position to take this opportunity by being prepared for it. Roman philosopher Seneca redefined the word luck with this quote below :

"Luck Is What Happens When Preparation Meets Opportunity." Seneca

Patience is essential in life, and especially on the journey of success. Once true patience is understood, then the journey of success can be more enjoyable than ever. This is because, even though we could want something to happen gravely. With patience, we can appreciate that nothing comes before it's time. This mindset is one of the focal points in having a healthy mindset during a successful journey.

"*Patience is the calm acceptance that things can happen in a different order than the one you have in mind.*"
David G. Allen

Patience also allows time to focus on our development. This development is a significant stage of preparation for a future opportunity. There is no quick fix for success and the most beautiful things in life take time. Value this time and the memories throughout this time because when all is achieved it's amazing to look back, be proud and reflect on the success you have earned.

"Give me six hours to chop down a tree and I will spend the first four sharpening the axe." Abraham Lincoln

Having the enthusiasm and overall aim to learn from every situation can be very advantageous. Lessons are present daily in our everyday lives. It's important to reflect and recognise what we can take from each day. We are constantly faced with different scenarios that we can use to understand our traits. For example, how we reacted to a situation, what was our body language, what words were used and how did we feel at the time. Learning our strengths and weaknesses as a person and ideally who we are daily is important because it gives a foundation for future growth. Finding and identifying these patterns in these scenarios is the first step. Becoming more self-aware and patient to learn more about yourself is something we are not always taught and therefore if it doesn't come naturally it may have grave effects on the level of success we achieve and the pain we can have along the journey due to the lack of growth.

Dealing with Stress

Every day we face additional stresses, and our attitude towards them makes all the difference. Stress is considered inevitable in life and it can cause mental, emotional strain or tension. Stress may arrive in various forms, such as worry, anxiety, fear, discomfort, and it's important to see it as a part of life. It essential to adopt a friendly attitude towards stress, and this develops our capacity when handling it.

Stress is not what happens to us. It's our response to what happens, and response is something we can choose.
- Maureen Killoran

When handling stress, we can start by becoming completely transparent with ourselves to have clarity in understanding our minds and our feelings.

With a viewpoint of your mind and feelings from the outside looking in, recognising what feelings you have and not identifying with any negative feelings. Almost viewing your feelings as if you are staring outside your bedroom window, eyes locked in on a passing car (The car representing your feelings) because just like a car passing, feelings can come and go. With a court-side view of our feelings, we can break the spell of emotionally reacting and the suffering that may follow. This detachment allows us to find coping methods that work for us as an individual.

when handling stress.

From a steady calm state to our worst memory we can understand the feelings that occur at peace and discomfort.

Fun fact:
Lobsters grow by moulting their hard exoskeleton, and they do so a lot: the average lobster can moult 44 times before it's a year old. By the time lobsters reach the age of seven, they moult once a year, and after that, once every two to three years, growing larger with each successive shedding of their exoskeleton.
As you contemplate handling stress in your life, think about the little lobster. When the lobster's shell becomes too confining, the

lobster feels uncomfortable and under pressure. It goes under a rocky shelf to protect itself, casting off its shell and producing a new one.

A healthy way to view stress is with an outlook that the current discomfort can be a prompt for change to come, and this is a healthy way to turn those negative feelings of worry into positive feelings of excitement. Stress isn't always bad some stress is proven to be good. Eustress is the term used for beneficial stress, psychological, and physical.

' Pressure makes diamonds'

"Everything negative (pressure, challenges) is all an opportunity for me to rise."
-Kobe Bryant

Changing our perception or how we interpret stress is a useful method of handling stress. We are encouraged to receive only good feelings and avoid difficult ones.

We need to understand that we usually take valuable lessons that we have learned during difficult, stressful times. Yes, it's helpful to have a support system when our stress is consuming us, however finding the strength to concur with our difficult stressful times ourselves can help mould a more resilient, wiser, and stronger version of ourselves.

It's very important that in times of stress on this journey of success we understand we are not alone. Seeking help is part of success, finding a mentor or someone we are comfortable voicing our thoughts in a time of stress is vital. If we ever feel down or in a negative space, we must have faith that this time will pass. Giving yourself time to rest and refocus is also crucial.

Having the ability to block out negative opinions is vital when dealing with stress. Understanding that someone's opinion isn't a fact and some people genuinely don't want you to succeed. Recognising that someones negative energy towards you, negative comment/opinion can be just out of pure hate. Humans are drawn to hatred and envy for many reasons. This isn't our problem and usually a problem they have within themselves which they are projecting on to you. It's very important to protect yourself by identifying these people because by becoming more aware we can learn that we should try our best to not attach our feelings or self-esteem to someone who has foul intentions.

One way of handling stress is to compartmentalise our problems. Dissecting every fear we have and finding the route to solving the stressful situation. The answers are there, whether internal or external. Sometimes by asking yourself if there are any solutions, other times by purely accepting that the stress will pass and time will be a healer. A mindset of acceptance for situations of our control is a true way to find peace during this trip of success.

Here's a list of stress reduction and coping methods

Exercise

When we exercise our heart rate increases, the blood flow to our brain also increases, exposing our brains to more nutrients and oxygen. Our body releases chemicals that make us feel happy such as dopamine, endorphins, serotonin and many more.

This can improve our mood and have a direct impact on decreasing our levels of stress.

Some chemicals that we release during exercise also help regulate our mood, giving us more control when dealing with stress.

"Training gives us an outlet for suppressed energies created by stress and thus tones the spirit just as exercise conditions the body." -Arnold Schwarzenegger

Meditation -

There are many types of meditation visualisation, mindfulness, transcendental, spiritual, focused, movement, mantra, progressive relaxation, loving-kindness

By Recognising what space we are in mentally, emotionally we should then research all forms of meditation and choose the type we feel may be beneficial to us.

"Meditation is the only way to freedom from stress, as it is a dimension beyond the mind. All the stress and struggle are of the mind." - Jaggi Vasudev

"Meditation, yoga, and walks are all ways to regulate our stress and reconnect." Arianna Huffington.

Socialising -

A problem shared is a problem halved - proverb

"Who needs a Stress reliever When you have your best friend aside." - Vemeera Krishnan

Self-care -

A change in our diet to healthier options can take away 'stress' because unhealthy foods affect our body and mind also developing a regular sleep routine.

'You are what you eat'

When discussing success, we usually focus on the outcome as if success is fixed. Success is never-ending. It's accomplishing a desired aim or result meaning even after we have achieved there is always something further. The common desires of success are usually wealth, fame, and social status however in our hearts we all know genuine success is the impact we have on others, when our name or existence is mentioned after we have passed, how will we be remembered. Success is in the memories we have of our lives, from the darkest times that we have overcome to the true growth and wisdom we've picked up throughout our journey. Success is found in the laugher during times of stress. Success is the inner will to get things done. Success is how you treat others and humility during times of victory. Success is found in times where we have failed and tried again without letting that failure get to our heart. Accepting failure is a part of the journey, using our experiences to learn is vital. Giving everything we have in our power to be the best version of ourselves possible.

<u>Success Ride</u>

The mounted weight on our shoulders is imaginary

The people we felt we've let down, are proud

Proud that we have tried

Proud we haven't given up

We have the strength to get up and go again

Next time it will be different

Now we know what else we need to do

Accept that it may not be the first or the

100th time

But we will achieve what we have set our

minds to achieve

Every day is a new opportunity to improve

A new opportunity to prepare

We won't waste time comparing ourselves

with others

Because we are unique in every way

Keep moving forward

We may surprise ourselves

We are closer than we think

The line can be a few steps away

And throughout this trip, we will find the

strength to smile

Smiling inside and out

We understand there is always a reason to

smile

We are grateful

Our stories are incredible

We are now the failure that is success!

"Success is no accident. It is hard work, perseverance, learning, studying, sacrifice and most of all, love of what you are doing or learning to do." Pele.

Printed in Great Britain
by Amazon

10030230R00047